W9-CNB-810

Simply SenseSational® Christmas

Simply SenseSational® Christmas

Simple, Beautiful Ways to Create a Cozy Home for Christmas

TERRY WILLITS

With photographs by Tim Olive

ZondervanPublishingHouse
Grand Rapids, Michigan

A Division of HarperCollins*Publishers*

Simply SenseSational® Christmas

Requests for information should be addressed to:

ZondervanPublishingHouse
Grand Rapids, Michigan 49530

Library of Congress Cataloging-in-Publication Data

Willits, Terry, 1959–
Simply SenseSational Christmas: simple, beautiful ways to create a cozy home for Christmas / Terry Willits : with photographs by Tim Olive.
p. cm.
ISBN: 0-310-21802-0 (hardcover)
1. Home economics. 2. Christmas decorations. 3. Christmas cookery. 4. Christmas sounds. 5. Christian life. I. Title. II. Title: Simply SenseSational Christmas
TX303.W567 1998
394.2663—dc21 98-10308
CIP

This edition printed on acid-free paper and meets the American National Standards Institute Z39.48 standard.

Published in association with the literary agency of Wolgemuth and Associates, Inc., 330 Franklin Road #135A-106, Brentwood, Tennessee 37027

Interior design by Sherri L. Hoffman

Printed in China

98 99 00 01 02 03 04 05 /❖ HK/ 10 9 8 7 6 5 4 3 2 1

To Jane Armstrong and Jenny Harden

Two angels on earth who introduced me

to the true meaning of Christmas

CONTENTS

INTRODUCTION

I love Christmas! Especially celebrating Christmas in my home. Yet coming to delight in the simple joy of Christmas has been a journey for me. A journey, quite frankly, I'm still traveling. Whenever I begin to think about an upcoming Christmas, I experience two emotions. First, there is the anticipation. Anticipation of special times with family and friends. Anticipation of the sentimental sights, sounds, smells, tastes, and touches of the season. Anticipation of the celebration of Christ's birth. Then, all too often, anxiety sets in. My mind shifts to the endless "to do" lists. I begin wondering how I can possibly get everything done — the decorations, the gifts, the cards, the cooking.

Though I've known since I was a child that Christmas is *really* about the birth of our Savior, as an adult I always felt that somehow I could obtain the "perfect" Christmas if I just worked hard enough. As a designer, I thought my house was supposed to be a picture-perfect showplace. I had visions of giving and receiving perfect presents, wrapped beautifully and tucked neatly under a perfectly shaped and decorated tree. As a writer, I felt obliged to send perfect Christmas cards with long, eloquent, handwritten letters. As a pastor's wife, I felt I needed to host perfectly delightful parties with delicious homemade goodies. And I was supposed to waltz gracefully through it all. Somehow, these fantasies never happened and I became weary of trying. One year in a moment of reflection, God showed me I was missing the mark of what he intended for Christmas — to simply rejoice in the gift of his Son.

This book has been born out of a desire to simplify the holidays in my own home, so I would have time to enjoy what really matters — celebrating Christ's birth with the people I love. Whether it's decorating my home, preparing a holiday meal, or wrapping a gift, I now stop and ask myself, "Is it simple? Is it necessary? Is there joy in my heart?"

I hope this book gives you permission to get back to the basics this Christmas. This is not a craft book or a family activity book. You won't need a master's degree in creativity or loads of time or money. All you need is a place you call home and a heart that wants to simplify the season there. The ideas within these pages are simple suggestions to inspire you with an "I can do that!" attitude. Don't feel they all need to be implemented; just a few tips will enhance your home and help you enjoy the Christmas season.

Wherever you are on your journey of joy for the holidays, I pray the pages that follow will encourage you to keep your Christmas at home

- *simple* — so you can enjoy the season, not just endure it
- *sense-filled* — so you can create a warm and welcoming home and wonderful memories for years to come
- *Christ-centered* — because Jesus Christ truly is the reason for the celebration

May God bless your home this Christmas with the simple joy and peace of his presence!

Terry

CHAPTER ONE

Making Sense of Christmas

The Christmas season is a festival for the senses.

Twinkling lights, the fresh scent of evergreen, a steamy mug of cider, jingling bells, a cozy fire; Christmas is the crowning highlight of every year! It is the celebration of the greatest gift ever given — God sending his Son to earth to redeem the world. And there's no better place than home to celebrate.

Home is the most powerful place on earth. It affects who we are and how we see the world. There's something about Christmas and home that go together. Maybe it's the sense of belonging, security, familiarity, and love. Or maybe it's having something constant in an ever-changing world. Even if the home you grew up in wasn't happy during the holidays, it is never too late to begin to make *your* home a positive place.

In my book *Creating a SenseSational® Home,* I introduced the simple concept of awakening the five senses to make your home warm and inviting, wherever you live. When our senses are stimulated in a positive way, any experience becomes more enjoyable. And the more senses stimulated at one time, the more memorable the experience becomes!

I'll be home for Christmas.

There is no better time than Christmas to fill our home with wonderful sights, smells, sounds, tastes, and touches. The same soothing smell of pine, the favorite holiday song, the predictable holiday feast, the familiar faces and voices of those we love. No doubt, these memories are what makes Christmas so sentimental.

When it comes down to it, relationships are the most important part of life. And the atmosphere we create in our homes at Christmas affects those relationships. God has given us as women an ability to influence our surroundings. When you walk into a home, you can sense the spirit of the homemaker. We are thermostats for our homes. We *set* the temperature. A joyful woman makes a joyful home. A stressed-out woman makes a stressed-out home. Our goal for this season should be to make home a place that reflects God's love.

Stick to simple ideas and apply them scrupulously.

— PIERRE PASCAL

It's easy to get so caught up in making things special at Christmas that we lose our joy. But God never asked us to "do it all." Instead, we need to simplify Christmas so that we can focus on others and the real reason for our celebration. If we do, the rewards will be rich. Filling our homes with a few easy touches that delight the senses will bring blessings to our loved ones this Christmas and for Christmases to come.

To simplify Christmas, it's necessary to prioritize what you can realistically accomplish. First, ask God to help you order your holidays and show you what's really necessary. Next, ask your family what means the most to them during the Christmas season. You'll probably be surprised to find you're putting undue pressure on yourself. Then, on a weekend in November, sit down with a notepad, pen, and your calendar and plan what you intend to do in your home this Christmas. When do you want to decorate, purchase the tree, wrap gifts, cook, send cards? Start early, so you can enjoy the season as it unfolds. Involve others with the duties and let go of perfectionistic expectations.

Simplify. Simplify.

— HENRY DAVID THOREAU

To have a simply "sensesational" Christmas, it is important to keep the main things the main things: Celebrating Christ, sharing life and love, making memories. So relax if you don't have money for a new sofa, or energy to transform your home into a winter wonderland, or time to make homemade fudge. Put on some holiday tunes, warm up some cider, light the tree, hug a loved one, and count your blessings. This Christmas, come back to your senses and keep it simple.

In the midst of making things "special," don't lose the simple.

— Rebecca Hayford Bauer

CHAPTER TWO

The *Sights* of Christmas

When they saw the star, they were overjoyed.

— Matthew 2:10

It was just a simple star, shining brilliantly in the pitch-black sky. But it was this lone beaming light that led the shepherds to the true Light of the World. When they saw the star with their own eyes, the shepherds abounded with joy and followed it to the baby Jesus. Here, they found the parents of the Christ Child celebrating his grand entrance into the world in a simple, humble stable. An undeniable spirit of joy and peace permeated the place. The shepherds sensed it and were glad they came.

Is that how others feel when they come into your home at Christmas? Simplicity often brings with it great joy and peace. A pine wreath hanging on the front door, glowing candles in the windows, fresh greenery laid leisurely atop the mantel — each is a simple, yet beautiful sight.

Certainly we want our homes to be a beautiful blessing during Christmas. Beauty attracts. Making our homes visually appealing for Christmas will hopefully draw others in so relationships can grow. But if decorating your home at Christmas is overwhelming or stressful to you, or if you feel obsessed to have every nook and cranny "perfect," simplify for your sanity.

Keep it simple. Keep your eyes on Him.

— Joni Eareckson Tada

Don't feel the need to overdo with Christmas decorations. Though many holiday magazines encourage extravagance, I believe the simplest decorations are the most striking. The eye can take in only so much at a time. If you want to create a peaceful home this season, your first step may be to clear some clutter, not add to it. Tuck away some of the things you look at every day.

To keep Christmas decorating simple, concentrate your efforts on four main areas of your home: the front door, the mantel (if you have one), the Christmas tree, and the table and chandelier where you plan to eat most of your holiday meals. Each of these focal points of your holiday can be decorated simply and beautifully. Decorating a few large areas will make more of a visual impact than scattering a few decorations in every room. If you have the time, energy, and desire to decorate other areas, go ahead — but keep in mind that people should be the priority for the holidays, not having a picture-perfect showhouse.

What goes up, must come down!

When decorating our homes at Christmas, we want to create a pleasant atmosphere where we can celebrate Christ's birth with those we love. Try to decorate with items that keep the focus on Christ's birth: a manger, angels, stars, lots of lights, and greenery. My eight-year-old nephew, Van, has his own manger scene (that was once his greatgrandmother's) to decorate his bedroom. He's learning at a young age that Christmas is about Jesus. Every year he anxiously anticipates displaying his manger pieces on his dresser.

Christ came to be a light in this dark world. Reflect his light this Christmas in your home with simple, special lighting. Any room can be enhanced by flickering candles, twinkling lights, an advent wreath, or spotlights.

Christ also came to give us everlasting life. Evergreens remind us of that fact as they bring life to our homes during the holidays. Greenery is a simple way to decorate inexpensively and beautifully. Take your garden snippers out back and cut some fresh greenery. In Atlanta, I cut pine branches, juniper, magnolia leaves, holly, and whatever else looks green and lively. Soaking greenery in a tub or wheelbarrow of water overnight will add moisture and allow greenery to last longer indoors.

When it comes to choosing colors for decorating your home at Christmas, there's nothing more Christmasy than the traditional red and green. In the Middle Ages, holly was used to decorate churches in England. The red berries signified the blood of Christ, and the prickly leaves, the crown of thorns. Gold has historical meaning as well (it was one of the generous gifts brought to the Christ Child by the wise men) and goes with many settings. If your home is pink or blue, decorate with colors that will enhance your environment, not distract from it — perhaps silver, raspberry, and deep blue. Most important, decorate with colors you enjoy.

Simplicity often brings with it great joy and peace.

1048

The more joyful the door, the warmer the hearth.

— DEB RINA

Simply SenseSational Front Doors

- A holiday mat will enhance your entrance and welcome friendly feet.
- Simple, white candles (electric or battery-operated) in your front windows will give an easy, elegant glow to your home's exterior.
- Luminaries, paper sacks filled with a votive candle and weighted down with sand, symbolize lighting the way to Bethlehem for Mary and Joseph. Make your sidewalk a welcome sight on Christmas Eve by lighting luminaries alongside it.

A festive front door can be as easy as an evergreen wreath with a spotlight shining brightly on it at night.

Simply SenseSational Mantels

Add whatever your heart fancies to mantel greenery, but keep it easy!

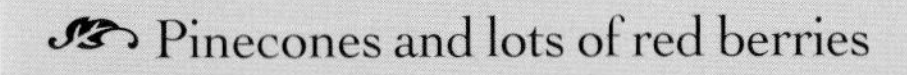

- Pinecones and lots of red berries
- Shiny Christmas balls and ribbon
- Fresh fruit: lemons, apples, oranges, pineapple, pomegranates
- Brass candlesticks and candles
- Stemmed glassware with votive candles
- Gift-wrapped empty boxes
- Decorative stockings hung with care

The mantel is a natural focal point at Christmas. Keep decorations for your mantel simple and beautiful. Clear off year-round accessories and create a base of greenery. Intersperse tiny white lights with a strand of garland, branches of evergreen, or magnolia leaves.

Christmas Tree, O Christmas Tree!

— E.G. Anschutz

Just as every home reflects the personalities and passions of the family who lives there, so should the Christmas tree! Decorate your tree with objects that have special meaning, but don't feel every branch needs to be laden with ornaments. Enjoy the simple beauty of the tree and glowing lights.

Simply SenseSational Christmas Trees

- Begin an ornament collection for each of your children.
- Top your tree with a big shining star to represent the Star of Bethlehem.
- Use inexpensive fillers to decorate your tree. Hang pinecones with raffia or tie lots of bows.
- Hang small saucers with plate hangers and hooks for a charming look.
- Add some friendly faces to your tree by hanging Christmas card photographs. Punch two holes in top of photo and thread with ribbon.

Food tastes better when there is beauty to behold.

Simply SenseSational Tablecloths

A pretty tablecloth is the foundation for a festive dining experience. Enjoy its beauty by keeping it on all season long. Christmas table coverings can be creative and reasonably priced.

- Decorative sheets or holiday fabrics (54" or wider) make easy tablecloths.
- Gather each corner of a tablecloth and tie with a ribbon for a special look.
- Try a white *matelassé* bedspread, or lace from a discount linen store.
- Toss a cotton or chenille throw over a small table or coffee table for a quick Christmas cover-up.

I am the light of the world.

— JOHN 9:5

A prominent lamp with a few holiday touches will give a special Christmas sparkle. Simply tie a bow or tassel around the neck and top the shade with a holiday finial, like an angel or star.

Crystal and silver can create an instant icy wintertime look for a centerpiece. For glitter, place pieces on a mirror or silver tray. Add tinsel, rock salt, or Ivory Snow flakes. Light candles for an elegant glow.

Shiny, colorful Christmas balls heaped in a bowl will dress up any spot. Light a candle nearby and watch its reflection dance merrily on the sparkling surfaces.

Simply SenseSational Plants

- Give a Christmas look to houseplants with big bows or tassels tied around their pots.
- Put twinkling white lights on large houseplants.
- Aim spotlights on plants in corners to cast an elegant shadow on the ceiling.

An attractive basket overflowing with a blossoming poinsettia is an easy decoration sure to bring life into your home throughout the holidays. Choose red, white, or pink poinsettias—whichever complements your color scheme. For visual interest, add a pot of trailing ivy and surround the plants with Spanish moss.

Simply SenseSational Collections

Collect something you love and put it on display during the holidays.

- Show off a Christmas village of houses and shops atop a snowy field of quilting batting.
- Give everyday collections a holiday look. Fill blue and white porcelain urns with greenery and berries. Dress up a teapot with a bow on its handle.

Heavenly angels gathered over the years hold special memories to their collector. Cluster collections together for visual impact.

Family and friends should be the focus of our time and energy at Christmas. Frame photos of Christmases past, clustering them where the family often gathers so all can reminisce. Or tack the streamers of a wired bow to the back of a frame for a quick Christmas look.

Away in a manger. No crib for a bed.

A manger scene placed in a strategic spot, like the entry hall table, will subtly remind all who pass by of the true reason for the season.

CHAPTER THREE

The *Fragrances* of Christmas

Then they opened their treasures and presented him with
gifts of gold and of incense and of myrrh.

— MATTHEW 2:11

Imagine walking up to your home. A whiff of the freshly cut pine wreath on the front door seems to say, "Come on in, it's Christmas here!" Stepping inside, the sweet scent of a cranberry candle greets you as it burns brightly on the foyer chest. The cozy, woodsy smell of a roaring fire in the fireplace draws you into the living room. Then you catch a wave of the fragrant Fraser fir towering in the corner of the room. As tempted as you are to curl up on the sofa and soak in these smells, irresistible aromas seep from the kitchen, luring you there. Cinnamon cider simmers on the stove, and a mouthwatering turkey roasts in the oven. There's no other place on earth you'd rather be!

If you truly want to tug on the heartstrings of loved ones this Christmas, then fill your home with wonderful smells. One of the most satisfying gifts you can give to anyone who enters your home this holiday season is pleasant fragrance.

One of God's sweetest gifts to us is our sense of smell.

Giving fragrance as a gift is not a new idea. After Jesus was born, the wise men brought the newborn babe three highly-valued gifts. Among these were frankincense and myrrh, both expensive fragrances. Just as the wise men worshiped and adored the Christ Child with their hearts and gifts, we can worship and adore Christ with our hearts and the gift of fragrance. Fancy, costly perfumes aren't necessary — just an open, servant heart and a few simple ways to scent our homes.

Fragrance is, without a doubt, my favorite sense to stimulate in the home, especially at Christmas! Simple, fast, and immediately satisfying, it might be the quick strike of a match as I light a cranberry-scented candle, a few drops of pine-scented fragrant oil in a lamp ring as I turn on a lamp, or a hasty shake or two of garlic salt and pepper on a roast before I pop it in the oven.

Smell is the most influential sense we possess. God wired up our noses to our brains so that the slightest smell can affect us. Fragrances stir our emotions and affect our behavior. The smell of peppermint perks us up and enhances concentration; the scent of pine or cedar soothes and calms. The more pleasant our environment smells, the more pleasant we are — reason enough to make our homes smell heavenly this holiday season!

Perfume and incense bring joy to the heart.

— PROVERBS 27:9

Don't underestimate the impact of filling your home with fragrance this Christmas. The blessings don't end when the fragrances do. Does the smell of gingerbread baking take you back to your grandmother's home at Christmas long ago? The fragrances that fill our homes today can be the memories that fill our minds tomorrow.

When selecting Christmas scents, let your nose be your guide. Fill your home with holiday fragrances that delight you. You may prefer the spicy smells of citrus, cloves, and cinnamon. Or perhaps you enjoy the sweet, fruity smells of apple, cranberry, or mulberry, or the woodsy smell of pine. For a more intense and unified fragrance, purchase several different products of the same Christmas scent, such as candles, room sprays, and potpourri. Or mix as you please. For me, the magical mixture of several holiday fragrances is what truly gives our house its unique "scent of home."

When I am expecting others to our home over the holidays, I like to make sure they smell some kind of enticing Christmas fragrance when they arrive. But I also bring fragrance into our home when I am all alone. I often light a deliciously scented candle as I sit and slow down from the holiday rush to be still before God. The quiet, fragrant flame calms my spirit and allows me to refocus on what really matters this holiday: my relationship with the Christ of Christmas and the loved ones he has brought into my life.

I secretly think that the real reason many of us love Christmas is because of the wonderful scents . . .

— Emelie Tolley

When I walk into a room and smell evergreens,
I think of Christmas . . .

— Leslie Linsley

The fresh, soothing scent of pine cannot be surpassed for filling your home with the smell of Christmas. Pine garlands draping your bannister, a fresh-cut Christmas tree, an evergreen wreath enhancing your front door, evergreen branches adorning your mantel, or a simple basket filled with bundles of pine all bring the enticing smell of greenery into your home.

Simply SenseSational Eucalyptus

Eucalyptus is an aromatic plant with an invigorating menthol scent. Try using it as additional fragrant greenery when decorating for Christmas.

- Tuck eucalyptus clusters in your Christmas tree branches for a fragrant filler. You can buy cranberry-colored eucalyptus or spray paint eucalyptus silver or gold. (Spray painting, however, will seal in the scent.)
- Hang a eucalyptus wreath on your showerhead. The steam from a hot shower will release the fresh scent!
- Eucalyptus is an especially fragrant wood. Decorate a jumbo eucalyptus log with a big bow and place it by your fireplace. Burn it on Christmas Day to fill your home with fragrance.

A large vase filled with eucalyptus, red berries, and spindly wood branches, makes an elegant and fragrant holiday decoration.

Hearth and home. The two go hand in hand.

Simply SenseSational Fireplaces

- Toss an armful of scented pinecones into a basket for a delightful Christmas fragrance.
- Place the pinecones beside a roaring fire in your fireplace; the heat of the flames will help release the scent.
- Occasionally toss a pinecone into the roaring flames for a burst of Christmas fragrance.
- Refresh the pinecones by adding a few drops of fragrant oil.
- A bag of scented pinecones tied with a big bow makes an inexpensive, "hearth-warming" gift!

The smell of a wood-burning fire evokes an immediate sense of warmth and security to any home at Christmas. If you have a fireplace, keep the flame burning and enjoy it often during the holidays.

The simple sparkle and smell of scented candles lends a warm holiday welcome.

A candle can pierce the darkest night.

Simply SenseSational Scented Candles

Scented candles can create instant atmosphere in your home at Christmas. The ways to display scented candles are limitless. Use your imagination!

- Light one by your back door before loved ones arrive home.
- Light a scented candle in your powder room for guests.
- Create beautiful candle holders with saucers, tea cups, glassware, or crystal bowls.
- Turn a silver bowl upside down for an elegant pedestaled candle holder.
- Surround a candle with cloves to release a spicy aroma.
- Line a stairway with scented votive candles in clear holders.
- Add a tablespoon of water to the base of votive candle containers to allow candles to be removed more easily. Or place votive glasses in freezer for fifteen minutes to make wax pop out without mess.

Guests will love having their own fragrant glitter at the table. At each place setting set a votive candle holder or pretty, stemmed glassware. Add scented votive candles and light.

A pretty handkerchief, square of Christmas fabric, or even muslin filled with a tablespoon of potpourri and tied with a tassel, ribbon, or twine, is the perfect touch to perfume any place. Use for party favors, doorknob decorations, or tree ornaments.

Simply SenseSational Sachets

Christmas-scented sachet envelopes can give your spirit a lift. Try cranberry, peppermint, frankincense, or evergreen.

- Surprise a loved one with a fragrant sachet in his or her pajama drawer.
- Stash an evergreen sachet in your coat closet for a fresh, outdoorsy smell.
- Tuck a sachet envelope under a bow or into a special Christmas greeting card.

Lamp rings are a safe and easy way to fill your home with a holiday scent. Place a lamp ring on a lamp's lightbulb, then add a few drops of fragrant oil, like pine, apple cinnamon, or cranberry. Turn the lamp on and enjoy the Christmas scent for hours.

Simply SenseSational Potpourri

- A scented candle in the middle of the potpourri bowl will create a doubly fragrant decoration.
- For the most aromatic potpourri, place it in a room's hottest spot, by a lamp or fireplace.
- A handful of potpourri tossed into a roaring fire will give a burst of Christmas scent to a room.

A few holly sprigs, a bright bunch of red berries, or scented pinecones give an instant holiday touch to potpourri. Add a few drops of Christmas-scented fragrant oil.

The right fragrance can bring a room to life.
— Claire Burke

A decorative bottle or can of holiday-scented spray in your powder room will invite friends and family to enjoy a quick spray of Christmas fragrance.

Stop and smell the spices.

— HELEN ISOLDE

A big bundle of cinnamon sticks tied with raffia makes an easy, scent-filled decoration or gift.

Simply SenseSational Cinnamon

- A simmering pot of water, cloves, cinnamon sticks, and orange peels on the stove will fill your home with a spicy Christmas aroma.
- Encircle a short pillar candle with double-face tape, then press cinnamon sticks vertically onto the tape. To hide the tape, tie ribbon or raffia around the sticks. The burning candle's heat will release the spicy scent.

A house becomes a home when good smells come from the kitchen.

A fresh orange covered with whole cloves lends a spicy holiday fragrance. Simply use a toothpick or nut pick to puncture fruit skin and insert cloves. A fun, fragrant project for kids!

The succulent smell of turkey roasting in the oven is guaranteed to make your home smell cozy and captivate family and friends until they get a taste.

CHAPTER FOUR

The *Tastes* of Christmas

Plan the Christmas menu knowing that the cook deserves a holiday too.

— HELEN ISOLDE

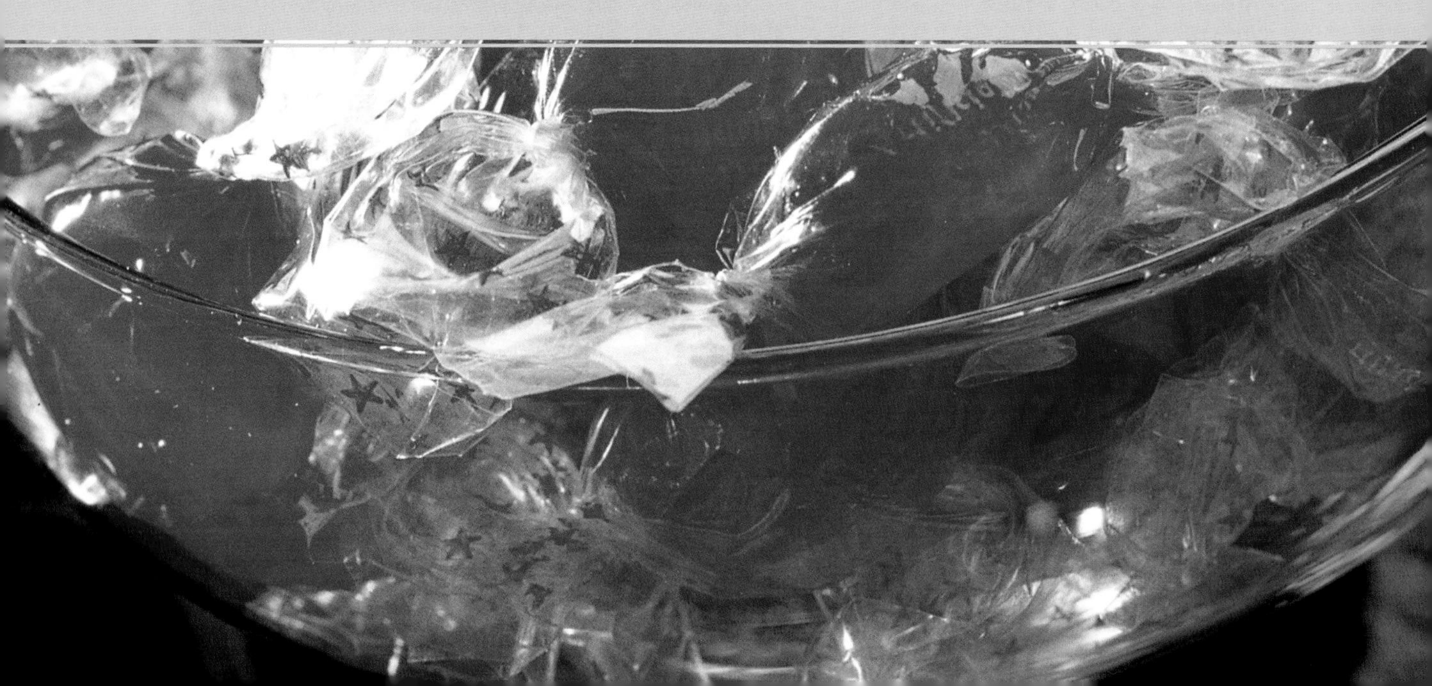

What would Christmas be without the tasty foods we often enjoy—turkey, dressing, delicious desserts, homemade candies? Appealing to the sense of taste in our homes during the holidays demonstrates perhaps the greatest labor of love to others. It's worth all the preparation just to watch my family or friends sit down to a meal I've prepared and see their great anticipation satisfied by that first bite.

To me, cooking at Christmas should be simple. If you have loads of time and love spending hours in the kitchen during the holidays, go for it and have fun sharing your delicacies! But if you are like many who have limited time and energy at Christmas, be encouraged. Filling your home with delicious food need not be a challenge. Simple, "sensesational" solutions provide tasty foods during this festive time.

They will rejoice in the bounty of the LORD . . .

—JEREMIAH 31:12

To save your sanity this holiday, sit down at the kitchen table with pen and paper and a hot cup of tea and take a few minutes to plan your meals. Good planning helps to make a stress-free Christmas. Hang a list on your refrigerator of menu options for which you have food on hand. Plan meals that are quick to prepare, taste great, and can be frozen and served more than once throughout the holidays. Chili, soup, and spaghetti all warm us up for the winter ahead.

Don't wait for the twenty-fifth of December to enjoy the mouthwatering taste of a holiday meat. Cook a ham or roast. Savor the smell and enjoy nibbling on it in the weeks before Christmas!

Though the holidays are often the time we splurge on goodies, try to prepare simple, healthy meals to counteract the temptations elsewhere. The better we eat anytime, the better we feel and the more energy we have. During the holidays, we need all the help we can get to be at our best!

I love to decorate our home at Christmas with the nutritious bounty of natural fruits God has made: a simple bowl of shiny apples, an orange studded with spicy cloves, a pineapple crowning a wooden bowl filled with red pears. Fresh fruit is lovely to look at as it adorns our homes during the holidays, and it is much easier to eat healthy when you have easy, tasty food on hand. Wander through the produce aisles of your grocery store and pick up some delicious Christmas decorations.

Traditions are . . . sweet memories that will last an entire lifetime.

— KAROL DEWULF NICHELL

Christmas traditions can play a big part when it comes to tantalizing the tastebuds. As children, we gathered around the tree every Christmas morning to open gifts. Without fail, my father would serve mugs of chilled eggnog sprinkled with nutmeg, just as his father did. I never cared too much for the taste of eggnog, but I couldn't pass up the tradition. So I'd take little sips of the sweet drink as we shared in one of the Christmas rituals that gave our family its unique heritage.

What are some of your tasty Christmas traditions? If you don't have any, start some this year. Let children or grandchildren help! I love to make homemade candy. My only prerequisites are that the recipes be easy and delicious. Most years, I whip up white chocolate bark and peanut clusters. They've become a family favorite and a Christmas tradition in our home. For a tasty Christmas card, enclose an easy recipe of a favorite holiday treat.

Why not prepare a favorite holiday dish from your childhood and savor the memories along with the great taste? I love to make my turkey stuffing just like my mother makes it, who makes it just like *her* mother made it. Last Christmas, my five-year-old niece Katy, had her first lesson with her grandmother on how to make our special stuffing. Maybe someday little Katy will be passing on this tasty legacy of love to her own family.

Recipes are like heirlooms handed down for generations.

— Carol Miller Radford

Traditions don't need to be saved for Christmas dinner only, though; make your Christmas Eve meal a tradition too. Clam chowder? Chili? Chinese food? Or what about ordering pizza the night you decorate the tree? Or for Christmas breakfast, a simple, make-ahead egg casserole and cinnamon rolls — anything that's simple and tasty. What makes traditions special is the sense of security and expectancy that comes from knowing "we are family and this is how we do it here!"

Christmas is a time of sharing the love and joy of Christ and caring for others. A natural way to do that is by opening your home. When practicing hospitality over the holidays, family and friends should be the focus, not the food. The secret is to keep it simple and prepare as much as possible in advance. When having people over, serve an easy make-ahead casserole, green salad, and bread. Or cater a part of your meal. Better still, have potluck and let everyone bring a dish. Ask friends to bring something that is traditional in their home. This will help them feel more "at home" in your home. Then relax and enjoy yourself. The more relaxed you are, the more relaxed everyone will be!

When it comes to sharing our home at Christmas, or any time of year, my prayer is that I bless, not impress. Whether I bless or impress has to do with my attitude as the hostess. To bless is to care for the needs of others — to put them at ease and to make them the priority. How can I do that if I am running around in the kitchen? To bless is also to open up my heart and my home just as it is, with no pretense. Trying to impress is what makes me stressed before others come, thinking, "Is my meal fancy enough? Is the house clean enough? How do my flowers look?" Me, me, me. I'm sure you've visited homes where the hostess has blessed and one where she has tried to impress. Ask God to help you be a blessing to those who come to your home this Christmas as you love and serve them.

Hospitality is about sharing a stress-free meal, not about serving a perfect meal.

Simply SenseSational Apples

- A hole in the top of an apple can hold a candlestick or tea lite candle.
- A small knife slit in an apple's top makes a perfect spot to hold a place card.
- Apple slices dipped in warm caramel sauce are a simple, sweet treat.

T's Easy Crispy Cobbler

(Simply delicious and yummy smelling! A "sensesational" dessert all winter long!)

Layer a greased 9 x 12 pan with sliced, peeled apples (or 2 cans cherry pie filling).

Top with a crumbled mixture of:

1 stick softened butter or oleo
1 cup flour
1 cup brown sugar

Cook at 350 degrees until crispy and bubbly. Serve warm with vanilla ice cream.

A bowl filled with red or green apples creates an economical and edible holiday decoration. Polish apples with a light coat of vegetable oil for a healthy luster. They will give your home a fresh, fruity scent and be a subtle reminder to eat healthy this season.

Simply SenseSational Pineapples

- Stand a pineapple in the center of a wooden bowl and surround it with red pears.
- When ripe and ready, slice up a pineapple and dip the juicy chunks in warm chocolate sauce.
- For a touch of glitter, spray paint a pineapple gold and stick a tapered candle firmly into the center of its leaves.

The pineapple has long been a sign of hospitality. A pineapple in a moss-lined pedestal urn creates an easy, hospitable mantel decoration for the holidays.

Some of the most simple and beautiful materials can be found in the grocery produce department.

— Jim Hartley

For a simply elegant statement, place a cranberry pillar candle on a saucer. Surround it with a hurricane globe and pour fresh cranberries around the candle. Or place cranberries in the base of a glass vase and then fill the vase with water and fresh flowers.

Real chocolate milk makes the fastest, tastiest hot chocolate of all! Microwave a quick mug of chocolate milk and top with marshmallows or swirl on a crown of whipped cream. Sprinkle with cinnamon sugar and slip in a candy cane. This sweet drink will tantalize the taste buds at any age!

Simply SenseSational Beverages

Preparing a holiday beverage for others is a gracious gesture that says "Merry Christmas!" in a tasteful way.

- Toast to the holidays with a hot mug of cider. Garnish with a cinnamon stick. For a quick and inexpensive alternative to apple cider, melt one cup of red-hot cinnamon candies in one gallon of apple juice. Leftover beverage can be chilled and reheated.
- Treat yourself to an afternoon cup of tea. Stir in a peppermint candy to wake you up. Open your Bible and reflect on God's Word as you sip.

Spicy tomato juice served warm in clear glass mugs with a celery stalk garnish is sure to put some zip into your festivities.

Simply SenseSational Service

Enjoy all of your home this Christmas. Varying your room settings for eating keeps life fresh and exciting.

- Move a small table into the den for a cozy feel.
- Serve a surprise snack on a small tray to kids in bed. When they fall asleep, sugar plums may just dance in their heads!
- Have a simple Christmas breakfast around the tree.
- Crawl into bed early one night with a mug of soup and crackers.

A wooden bowl filled with a variety of nuts invites anyone to sit down and crack open a healthy holiday snack. For function as well as a festive look, have a nutcracker soldier stand guard beside the bowl.

We are drawn to warmth. So dine where it's cozy!

There's no cozier place to dine than in front of a fire with the lights dimmed. Clear off the coffee table and eat beside the glowing Christmas tree.

The best kind of onion soup is the simplest kind.

— Ambrose Bierce

French Onion Soup

(A simple and inexpensive favorite in our home)

8 medium onions, sliced
16 beef bouillon cubes
8 cups water
Cooking sherry (optional)
8 slices Swiss cheese
8 slices of bread

Sauté onions in butter. Add beef bouillon cubes and water. For extra flavor, add a splash of cooking sherry. Heat well. Lay a slice of bread and Swiss cheese in the bottom of each soup bowl. Top with hot soup. Serves 8.

A big bowl of hot soup will warm you on a crisp winter night. Master one easy soup and make a huge pot of it. Try a favorite, like French Onion. Eat some, freeze some, and share some. For an easy, hearty dinner, serve soup and sandwiches.

Prepare simply. Present beautifully.

A roast is an easy, affordable way to feed a crowd for Christmas. Pierce the meat well and marinate it with Italian dressing overnight in the refrigerator. Or purchase an already marinated package of pork loin roast or pork tenderloin from your meat department. Pop the roast in the oven and cook until juicy and tender. Your house will smell delicious, and the meat will melt in your mouth.

Prewashed greens, sliced red onions, crumbled blue cheese, and toasted pecans all drizzled with Christmas Cranberry Vinaigrette makes a simply delicious accompaniment to any holiday meal.

Christmas Cranberry Vinaigrette

(A quick holiday taste for salads!)

1/4 cup oil
1/2 cup fresh cranberries
1/2 cup rice vinegar
3 T. Mrs. Dash seasoning
3 T. sugar

Mix in blender.

Simply SenseSational Sweets

- Toast marshmallows over a hot fire.
- Fold down a loved one's bedsheets. Secretly place a Christmas candy on his or her pillow.
- Mix red or green colored sugar crystals with white granulated sugar to enhance a simple bowl of sweetness.

. . . just a little something sweet to eat.

A pretty tasseled or ribboned jar filled with Christmas candies invites anyone with a sweet tooth to lift the lid and enjoy.

A store-bought angel food cake, frosted with a mixture of 2 cups Cool Whip topping and 8 oz. softened cream cheese and sprinkled with coconut, creates a stress-free dessert to celebrate Christ's birth. Garnish with greenery and a red cherry. Refrigerate until ready to serve.

Wrap clusters of white chocolate bark in clear cellophane and tie with a big bow. Find a simple food you enjoy preparing and make it your trademark Christmas gift to share with others. No time to cook? Buy something delicious and wrap it up beautifully!

White Chocolate Bark

2 pounds white chocolate
2 cups pretzel sticks
2 cups salted peanuts

Melt chocolate slowly in microwave. Stir in nuts and pretzels. Spread thinly on wax paper. Cool and break into random-sized pieces.

Simply SenseSational Helpers

Letting kids pitch in with the cooking can create Christmas fun and make lifelong memories.

- Roll out refrigerator cookie dough. Let kids cut their favorite Christmas shapes. Bake cookies. Frost and decorate with sprinkles.
- Construct quick gingerbread houses by adhering frosted graham crackers to paper milk cartons. Decorate with candies.
- Have children hand deliver Christmas goodies to neighbors.
- Let older children handwrite the Christmas dinner menu or input it into a computer and make copies. Roll them up and tie with a ribbon by each place setting.

CHAPTER FIVE

The *Sounds* of Christmas

I bring you good news of great joy that will be for all the people.

—LUKE 2:10

Listen. A gentle whimper, then contented coo of the newborn baby Jesus as Mary rocks him in her arms. The neigh of a nearby donkey. The baa of a little lamb lying at Joseph's feet. The munch of hay from a hungry horse outside the stable. The awesome silence of a star-filled sky. These were the soothing sounds of the first Christmas. Indeed, there was peace on earth.

In some fields not too far off, shepherds were watching wearily over their flocks. Ready to call it a day and set up camp, they were unrolling their blankets to settle under the stars for some silent sleep. Suddenly the peaceful quiet of the blackened skies exploded with blazing lights and the amazing appearance of an angel. Abounding with joy, the angel announced that Christ the Savior had been born! Then a whole choir of heavenly angels filled the skies and praised God, singing, "Glory to God in the highest! And on earth peace to men!"

The hearts of the once-weary shepherds were now racing. They stood silent and stunned for a moment. Then, with exhilarative shouts to one another, packed up camp and hurried to follow the star to see the Savior.

From the tranquil sounds of the stable to the jubilant sounds of the angels, a myriad of emotions were experienced that evening. And the sounds that filled the skies

Silent night, holy night,
All is calm, all is bright.

—JOSEPH MOHR

reflected those feelings of peace, contentment, gratefulness, wonder, shock, excitement, and awe.

Today we can experience many of those same emotions at Christmas. The walls of our homes should reflect the sounds of our heartbeat. For a truly harmonious holiday, both soothing and joyful sounds should fill our homes.

Sing, choirs of angels, sing in exultation.

—JOHN FRANCIS WADE

The joyful sounds of bells ringing, loved ones laughing, carolers singing, and upbeat music playing bring life and energy to the home. Almost every year, Bill and I have a white elephant Christmas party in our home. Guests are asked to wrap up the silliest, tackiest gift they can find around their house. Each person selects a wrapped gift and opens it in front of all. Last Christmas, I laughed so hard my jaw hurt. Our home was truly filled with the joy and laughter of friends.

During the Christmas rush, make the most of mealtimes. Take every opportunity to sit down and eat together. It's not as much about the food as it is about fellowship. Linger at the table. Put a basket nearby with Christmas cards you've received from friends. After the meal, read a holiday note and reminisce about that relationship. Some of my favorite memories of Christmas are of family gathered around the table after a meal, sipping coffee, telling embellished stories of the past, laughing, and sharing life with each other.

Have family and friends bundle up and go caroling in your neighborhood one evening. Or invite friends in and sing Christmas carols to get everyone in the holiday spirit. If you have a piano, let someone play as you all sing Christmas songs. Every year the whole Willits family gathers for Christmas, we surround my sister-in-law, Suzi, and sing as she tickles the keys with her talented touch.

Bring harmony to your home this holiday.

While jubilant sounds create a spirit of celebration, soothing sounds create a spirit of peace in our homes. A crackling fire, heartfelt prayers around the table, the words "I love you," and quiet solitude alone with God, for example, all are peaceful, quiet sounds that soothe the soul and speak to the heart.

At least one night this Christmas season, when the kids are in bed, turn off the television and enjoy the precious sound of silence. Take in the beautiful silence of a snowfall or a quiet, starry night. Sit on the sofa and talk with a loved one, or read a book in front of a crackling fire with no more sound than the turning of a page.

The most important sound of all is the words that flow from our lips. Make your time alone with God a priority this season. As you do, your days will be divinely ordered and your home will be filled with the most pleasing sound of all at Christmas — the loving words flowing from a Christ-filled heart.

The loving, holiday spirit in your home depends more on the words you speak than on the gifts you give.

— H. JACKSON BROWN

Simply SenseSational Bells!

Jingle those bells! For simple, sound-filled decorations, use bells everywhere.

- Tie big, bowed bells to refrigerator, microwave, and oven door handles.
- Ring a hand bell when Christmas dinner is ready.
- Punch a hole in place cards or name tags and thread a ribbon through the hole. Tie a bell to the ribbon.
- Put a big bell on your key chain to avoid misplacing your keys in the holiday rush.
- Hang bells on some bottom branches of your Christmas tree so you'll hear when little hands or paws are in the decorations or gifts.

Whenever you hear a bell . . . remember that Jesus came to make us free, not just in our country, but in our hearts.

—Rebecca Hayford Bauer

A lovely bell or string of bells tied with a ribbon or tassel to entry doorknobs is a quick Christmas decoration. The jingle will signal anyone coming or going and become a familiar holiday greeting to family.

A jingle bell pillow is a fun way to make your sofa sound "sensesational" for Christmas. Simply pin or stitch a big bell on each corner of a pillow. Jingle bell pillows make great, unique gifts!

I heard the bells on Christmas day . . .

—HENRY WADSWORTH LONGFELLOW

A Christmas bell on your dog or cat's collar will put even the family pet in the spirit of the season as he or she prances around your home.

Music makes life a symphony when God is the conductor.

A charming Christmas music box adorns a tabletop and invites the curious passerby to open and enjoy a holiday melody.

Simply SenseSational Music

Filling our homes with favorite Christmas songs creates instant atmosphere and a festive spirit. Make your home merry with music this season.

- Give praise to the Lord as you listen to songs that sing of the miracle of Christ's birth and life.
- Put on peaceful Christmas music after a stressful day.
- Each year, add a new CD or cassette to your collection of Christmas music.
- Play an old favorite holiday album and reminisce about Christmases past as you pull out your decorations.
- Use musical instruments to decorate. Thread decorative trumpets or french horns with tassels and greenery.

And heaven and
nature sing. . . .

— Isaac Watts

The sweet sounds of nature, such as birds singing outside your kitchen window, can be soothing during the holiday season. Attract birds by decorating an outdoor tree with edible goodies, like unsalted pretzels or bagel halves spread with peanut butter and dipped in birdseed. The birds will love their festive feast. Listen as they sing their praises!

There is no place more delightful than one's own fireplace.

The snap, crackle, and pop of burning logs in a fireplace is a cozy Christmas sound that says, "Come on in!" To guarantee your wood will be seasoned before burning, have wood delivered at the end of each winter for burning the following fall/holiday season. Toss some pinecones into a roaring fire for an extra pop!

Advent means "coming," and an advent wreath will help anticipate Christ's coming all season long. This wreath of greenery has four candles, each symbolizing an important aspect of Christ's birth, and a fifth central candle celebrating his birth. Beginning with the Sunday after Thanksgiving, light the first candle. Each consecutive Sunday, light an additional candle. On Christmas Eve, light the final candle. To enhance the meaning of advent, read aloud with your family passages from the Old Testament that prophesy the coming of the Messiah. Then read the corresponding New Testament passage that shows the fulfillment of each promise.

First Sunday — The Prophecy Candle
Read: Isaiah 7:14; 9:6–7; Luke 1:30–35

Second Sunday — The Bethlehem Candle
Read: Micah 5:2; Luke 2:1–7

Third Sunday — The Angel's Candle
Read: Isaiah 52:7; Luke 2:8–14; 4:18–19

Fourth Sunday — The Shepherd's Candle
Read: Ezekiel 34:23; Luke 2:15–20; John 10:11

Christmas Eve — Christ's Candle
Read Isaiah 9:2; Luke 2:30–32

On Christmas Eve, read the Christmas story in its entirety (Luke 2:1–20) with your family. Afterward, talk about the emotions of that precious night. Then pray, thanking God for the gift of his Son.

It is in my quietest moments that God speaks the loudest.

Take time this Christmas to find a cozy corner and be alone with God. Spend time reading his Word. Let God order your holidays. Try to get up early to read the Bible, write in a journal, and pray. As you spend time in quiet solitude, God will clearly lead you through the holidays with his peace and priorities.

HAGGAI
PROVERBS
1 KINGS
PSALMS
MARK
JONAH
JEREMIAH
EZRA

CHAPTER SIX

The *Touches* of Christmas

She wrapped him in cloths and placed him in a manger.

—Luke 2:7

My favorite thing to do on a winter night is to crawl into bed. The simple pleasure of this small act cannot be surpassed. Slipping under the smooth sheets and layers of familiar-feeling blankets and nestling my head into clouds of Christmas-cased pillows piled high — it's heaven! I feel safe and secure in my own little world.

I wonder if that's how the newborn baby Jesus felt when Mary wrapped his tiny, bare body in soft cloths and nestled him in the hay-lined manger. I'm sure he felt safe and secure in his new world. After all, it was *his* world. The God of all Comforts came to this earth as a child and experienced for himself loving human touch.

Come and behold him.
— JOHN FRANCIS WADE

Christmas is about giving. Touch is about giving, too. And touch is a precious gift to give in our homes at Christmas. Just as Mary gave Jesus her tender touch, we can share loving touches to make our homes a place of comfort this holiday. A place that draws others in. A place where people want to stay. A place where relationships grow and flourish.

God wired our bodies so that we actually *need* physical touch to live happy, healthy lives. With the busyness of the holidays, we need to slow down and take time to treasure touch in our homes. Hug family and friends as we greet them in the doorway. Clasp hands as we pray before a meal. Hold someone who is hurting. Cuddle with kids. Hang a few sprigs of holly with a bow on your front hallway ceiling light as a kissing bough. I cannot remember one wrapped gift my sweet grandmother ever gave me, but I still recall those big, bear hugs and kisses she gave us at her front door every Christmas!

Fluffy, festive pillows and cozy blankets are wonderful material touches that make our homes warm and welcoming at Christmas. While I was growing up, my mother made Christmas pillowcases for us. I couldn't wait to pull out my Christmas pillowcase, slip it over my pillow, and sleep on it. Each night, as I crawled in bed and my head hit the pillow, my mother's touch of love reminded me Christmas was near.

Several years ago, I bought simple stripe and polka dot fabrics in Christmas colors. (You can also buy ready-made pillowcases and decorate them with permanent markers). I am not a seamstress, but I stitched up some quick Christmas pillowcases for my nieces and nephews. When the whole family gathers at Christmas, it's fun to see the kids roll out of the vans with their Christmas pillows in hand. Our tradition of Christmas touch carries on!

Another holiday highlight for me is keeping in touch with faraway friends through Christmas cards. I love opening the mail this time of year. I sit down with my letter opener in hand, slide open the seams of red, green, and white envelopes, slip out the contents, and catch up with friends. It's so much fun to see how they have changed and to hear what God is doing in their lives.

God loves a cheerful giver.
— 2 CORINTHIANS 9:7

You can share the same joy with others this season from your home by sending a simple card. It can even been a pretty postcard. To me, sending Christmas cards allows us to give a touch of love to those too far away to hug. When I send Christmas cards, I try to make the experience as satisfying as possible. I'll sit on a floor pillow at our pine coffee table in front of a crackling fire, scented candle burning, hot chocolate close by, and Christmas music playing. I'll jot a quick line or two to dear friends with my favorite red felt pen in hand. As I do, I think about the way our lives have touched and thank God for them.

When it comes to gift giving and wrapping, keep it simple! It's easy to get so focused and frantic over the gifts themselves that we forget about the giver of all good gifts — God — and the gift he gave us in his Son.

I have a gift closet/wrapping area in our home that makes gift giving easy and pleasurable. The more convenient something is, the more apt we are to do it! I store all my wrapping necessities here. I even keep a few extra little gifts on hand. When someone invites us to their home over the holidays, I can whip them up something from my closet of goodies — a fragrant candle, cider mix, or a Christmas CD. A white gift bag, a fluff of colorful tissue, a quick tulle bow, and *Voila!* A simple, "sense-sational" gift!

You and I should be the best gifts that we could ever give one another.

— JONI EARECKSON TADA

After the time and energy spent on gift selecting and wrapping, we need to enjoy the giving and receiving of gifts. For a special touch of love, let everyone open one gift on Christmas Eve. (Maybe new pajamas to sleep in that night!) Then, Christmas morning, cherish the once-a-year time together of gift giving. Who cares how long it takes? Put on some holiday music, prepare a special beverage, and enjoy one another. After all, some of the greatest gifts we have are already opened.

The week between Christmas and New Year's is usually a bit more peaceful. Start a Christmas memory album or journal as a keepsake for the holidays. Write in it while your memories are still fresh. Record the highlights so you can look back and treasure the memories in years to come. Describe the sights, smells, sounds, tastes, and touches of celebrating Christmas in your home. They will become loving memories that will last a lifetime. Also, take a few minutes and dash off a note of thanks to those who gave you gifts. Gratitude should be the attitude of our hearts.

Beauty draws you in. But comfort keeps you there.

Simply SenseSational Pillows

- Tie an everyday decorative pillow with a pretty tassel, tulle, or wide wired-ribbon bow.
- Have a family Christmas slumber party sleeping in front of the tree. Pile all the bed pillows and blankets you can find. Pop popcorn and snuggle close. Sweet dreams!

Christmas needlepoint pillows will bring a tasteful holiday touch to your home. Pull them out every year and toss onto a sofa or armchair for simple, stress-free decorating. A cozy throw or quilt draped over the sofa is a comforting invitation to stay awhile. Curl up under one as you read a book or magazine or watch an old Christmas movie.

Simply SenseSational Christmas Cards

Keeping in touch with friends is one of the joys of Christmas.

- Let kids help design the card. Make copies on red or green paper. Let them stuff and seal envelopes, and put on stamps.
- Save time keeping in touch by writing a brief, one-page family newsletter. Make copies and enclose with each Christmas card.
- Keep one copy of the card and letter you send out each year. Compile them in an album and set it out on the coffee table to reminisce.
- If it's an especially difficult or hectic holiday, skip the cards this Christmas or send them on Valentine's Day!

A clear punch glass makes a simple napkin ring and gives a touch of Christmas charm to each place setting. Thread a napkin through the glass's handle and tie a place card to it with ribbon. Place a votive candle in the cup.

Make new friends. But keep the old. One is silver. The other is gold.

Large evergreen leaves as place cards give place settings a personal, natural touch. Write guests' names in gold marker on the leaves.

Simply SenseSational Place Settings

- Tie silverware and holiday napkins together with wired ribbon bows.
- For a casual look, tie silverware with a few strands of raffia and a sprig of greenery. Toss in a basket for guests to serve themselves.
- Use pretty paper Christmas napkins, plates, and cups for quick clean-up. Stock up when they're on sale.
- Write guests' names with gold marker on shiny Christmas balls for festive place cards and party favors.

Carving the holiday turkey should be cause for celebration!

An excellent sharp knife makes slicing holiday meat a joy! Assure certain knives are sharp before the holiday feasting begins. Many grocery store butchers will sharpen knives at no charge. For effortless carving, use a sharp electric knife.

A bow-tied dining chair is a simple, inexpensive touch that will warmly welcome any guest to your table. Tie bows on everything! If your fingers fumble when it comes to bow making, try using big spools of tulle net, wired ribbon, tassels, or natural strands of raffia. All are simple to tie and look beautiful. If all else fails, buy ready-made bows or use the self-adhesive bows. Remember, keep it simple!

Wrapping all of your gifts in white paper will keep your holidays simple and stress-free. Similarly wrapped gifts will lend a signature touch and will look wonderful nestled under the tree. Rather than fussing with tags, write directly on the gift with a nice marker, or write on the ribbon from the bow.

Let it bow! Let it bow! Let it bow!

Simply SenseSational Gifts

- Tuck a sprig of pine or eucalyptus under a bow for a fragrant touch.
- Tie a candy cane, cinnamon sticks, or a pretty tea bag to a bow for a tasty touch.
- For a Christmas jingle, tie a bell to a gift.
- Wrap up empty boxes beautifully as inexpensive decorations. Put them above kitchen cabinets, atop an armoire, on bookshelves, across the mantel, or use as a table centerpiece.
- Fill a gift basket with little gifts for each of the senses: a scented candle, Christmas music, peppermint tea bags, holiday beverage napkins, and a tree ornament. Wrap the basket with cellophane and a fluffy bow.

Seek rest.

— Helen Isolde

Simply SenseSational Bath Touches

- Tickle your body with foaming bubbles.
- Relax in a lukewarm bath before company comes.
- Roll up a towel to rest your neck.
- For a good night's sleep, sit, soak, and soothe your weary body right before you turn in for the night. Close your eyes and thank God for the good things this Christmas.

A long, hot bath is a great gift to give yourself to slow down and relieve stress this season. For extra touches, fill a basket with soaps, lotion, powder, sponges, and brushes and keep it close at hand.

CHAPTER SEVEN

The *Heart* of Christmas

Let every heart prepare Him room.

— Isaac Watts

So, Christmas is around the corner! Hopefully, you feel inspired to enhance your home simply and "sensesationally" this holiday season. In the preceding sections, I shared easy ways to make our homes warm and welcoming for Christmas. We want to keep Christmas simple so we have time to enjoy the season with those we love. We also want to make our homes sense-filled, so that they are a pleasant place where memories are made.

But the truth is, Christmas is about more than what we see, smell, taste, hear, or feel. Though all of these experiences make Christmas special and sentimental, none of them are the heart of Christmas. Somewhere along the way, from that stable over two thousand years ago to today, Christmas has become complex. Yet God's intent for Christmas is very, very simple. It should bring us joy, peace, and hope, not stress.

The best gifts are tied with heartstrings.

God has a very precious and valuable Christmas gift for each of us. Although his gift is modestly wrapped, the contents can change our lives forever. God's gift costs us nothing. It's the gift of his Son. John 3:16 explains the heart of Christmas very clearly. "For God so loved the world [that includes all of us!] that he gave his one and only Son [Jesus Christ], that whoever believes in him [receives God's gift of Christ as Savior] shall not perish but have eternal life [live with him forever in heaven!]."

A gift only becomes ours once we have received it. Is God's gift to you still hiding humbly under all those pretty packages beneath your tree? If so, Jesus Christ could be the greatest gift you ever received. He wants to be born anew in your heart.

As a child, after the stockings were unloaded, the gifts opened, the turkey gobbled down, I laid out all my gifts on the bed. I still recall feeling disappointed, thinking, *This is it? This is what I've been waiting for? And now it's over!* Later in life, I learned there is more to Christmas. I understood that God sent his Son, Jesus, to have a relationship with me and fill the hole in my heart that couldn't be satisfied by anything else on earth.

This holiday season, have fun filling your home with glimmering lights, simmering scents, tasty treats, soothing sounds, and cozy touches; but as you do, don't miss the Christ of Christmas. For he truly is the heart of it all!

Remember that peace on earth starts with peace in our homes and in our hearts.

— H. Jackson Brown

ACKNOWLEDGMENTS

A heartfelt thanks to:

- Tim Olive for sharing your gift of photography to make these pages come to life.
- Mike Blackwell for your faithful and professional assistance with the photo shoots.
- Brenda Jones for the endless errands and encouragement throughout our shoots.
- Sandy VanderZicht for believing in this project and the ministry of SenseSational® Homes.
- Rachel Boers for fine-tuning my words with your skillful editing.
- Sherri Hoffman and Jody Langley for your creativity and perseverence to make this book the best it could be.
- The Olives, Dunns, and Ryans for sharing their homes.
- My precious husband, Bill—for encouraging me through yet another book-writing project.
- You, my friend, for taking the time to read this book. May God bless your home this season as you seek to know the Christ of Christmas!

For information about Terry Willits' speaking schedule and SenseSational®
Homes products, please send a self-addressed, stamped business envelope to:

SenseSational® Homes, Inc.
P.O. Box 70353
Marietta, GA 30007

CREATING A

SenseSational

HOME

TERRY WILLITS

Awaken the senses to bring life & love to your home.

Creating a SenseSational® Home

Awaken the senses to bring life & love to your home

TERRY WILLITS

Lord, each sense that I have
Is a blessing from above.
May I celebrate your goodness
As I fill my home with love.

Wherever you live, your home can be a warm and welcoming place. In this beautiful book, Terry Willits shows you how to bring a fresh dimension of life and love to your home by awakening your five God-given senses.

As an interior designer, Terry knows there is more to making a home appealing than just pleasing the eye. In *Creating a SenseSational Home,* she offers a uniquely balanced perspective, combining both physical and relational ways to enhance your home's atmosphere through sight, smell, taste, sound, and touch. You will impact not only your family, but also your friends and other guests who visit; they will feel comfortable and welcome in your home.

Terry walks you room by room through your home to inspire you with fun, wise, and affordable ideas:

- Basic but beautiful decorating tips, from discovering your personal style to simple accessorizing
- Easy ways to fragrance your home, using a bouquet of flowers, a scented lamp ring, a lemony-scented sachet
- Simple ways to tease the tastebuds, from a cup of tea to a sweet treat on a bed pillow
- Encouraging hints for filling your home with pleasant sounds, including the gentle tick of a clock and the tone of your own voice
- Practical tips for bringing touches of comfort, from warm hugs to cozy pillows or cool glasses of water

In short, easy-to-read sections filled with simple hints, tips, and watercolor illustrations, here is how you can make your home a relaxing, inviting, and refreshing haven—a place you'll love to return to and where others will love to linger.

Hardcover 0-310-20223-X

We want to hear from you. Please send your comments about this book to us in care of the address below. Thank you.

ZondervanPublishingHouse
Grand Rapids, Michigan 49530
http://www.zondervan.com